Selchan

From Trails to Turnpikes

Tim McNeese

Crestwood House
New York

Maxwell Macmillan Canada
Toronto

Maxwell Macmillan International
New York   Oxford   Singapore   Sydney

Design: Deborah Fillion
Illustrations: © Chris Duke

Crestwood House
Macmillan Publishing Company
866 Third Avenue
New York, NY 10022

Maxwell Macmillan Canada, Inc.
1200 Eglinton Avenue East
Suite 200
Don Mills, Ontario M3C 3N1

Macmillan Publishing Company is part of the
Maxwell Communication Group of Companies

First Edition

Printed in the United States of America

10 9 8 7 6 5 4 3 2 1

Library of Congress Cataloging-in-Publication Data

McNeese, Tim.
    From trails to turnpikes / by Tim McNeese. — 1st ed.
        p.   cm. — (Americans on the move)
    Includes bibliographical references.
    Summary: Traces the history of American roads, from early paths created by the buffalo and the native Americans, to the city streets and highways of today.
    ISBN 0-89686-731-5
    1. Roads—United States—History—Juvenile literature. [1. Roads—History.] I. Title. II. Series: McNeese Tim. Americans on the move.
    HE355.M4   1993
    388.1'0973—dc20   91-41352

★

Contents

★

Introduction

Today, travel in the United States is easy. Automobiles take people to as many places as they want to go. City streets and rural roads connect neighbors, friends and local businesses. Highways connect states, allowing travelers to move across the entire nation with ease. Roads and highways crisscross the country and even link automobile, truck and bus traffic to other nations. Today's traveler often thinks of a trip in terms of minutes and hours, rather than miles.

But for travelers in early America, getting from one place to another was never easy. People at that time used different means of transportation from what most of us use today. In America's earliest days, roads

did not exist. European colonists first used trails and paths created by buffalo and the native Americans. Many people either rode a horse or walked from place to place, even over long distances. Boats were frequently used to take settlers up and down river systems.

Over time, however, colonists and pioneers began to develop their own land transportation system. They created new trails and paths. They built new roads, allowing settlements to spread across the continent. Such roads allowed the young American nation to grow quickly. This book is not only about those pioneers who moved across the land to the West but about the routes, old and new, that helped early settlers get around.

The development of early roads and trails was an exciting part of American transportation history.

★

Herds of buffalo were responsible for creating the earliest trails in America.

America's First Road Builders

When the first Europeans came to America, they found a land thick with ancient forests. Trees had rarely been cut down by the native Americans, so these woods had grown for hundreds of years untouched by humans. Many of the trees were huge. Their trunks might measure as much as 10 to 15 feet across. Often the trees were covered with vines and other plant growth, making the forests dark and gloomy.

From the Atlantic Ocean to beyond the Mississippi River, the land was covered with trees. Only in parts of Indiana, Kentucky and Illinois was the forest pattern broken. This great wilderness ran 1,000 miles east and west and the same distance north and south. Much of this forest remained unspoiled even after the arrival of the European immigrants. As late as 1800, great tracts of forest land had never heard the sound of the axe.

The Buffalo

But even these thick forests were covered with paths and trails. The earliest trails were made by the buffalo. Long before the American Indian came to the continent, great herds of buffalo had roamed the land that would someday be the United States. These animals could be found east and west of the Mississippi River. The buffalo trails were often very wide "highways." Large herds cut wide paths through forest areas in the East. These animal trails often led to the best fords (shallow places for crossing a river), **salt licks** and rich, green meadows. Frequently, such buffalo roads indicated the shortest distance between two points. These trails were very well marked. Some of them had been used for so long that the buffalo had worn ruts several feet deep into the ground.

American Indian Paths and Trails

By the 1600s, nearly 300,000 American Indians lived in the area from the Atlantic Ocean to the Mississippi River. They formed many different tribes or nations, from the Great Lakes to Florida. Often these nations stayed in contact with each other. They sometimes used the large river systems for travel by canoe, but most long-distance travel was done on foot. The native Americans often used the buffalo trails to travel from place to place. Over time, the native Americans created trails of their own. These paths were often very different from the broad buffalo roads. Usually an Indian trail was between 12 and 18 inches wide. Natives traveled the trail in single file. Some of these paths were used by so many native Americans for so long that their moccasins wore foot-deep ruts into the ground. Such tracks were used by runners who delivered messages between friendly tribes. These tribal messengers could sometimes cover 100 miles a day on the trails, running from sunrise to sunset.

Like the buffalo trails, the Indian paths often followed the best routes between destinations. These trails cut across bends in rivers, making the distance

By building paths and trails, native American tribes were able to communicate with each other.

★

shorter. They avoided the tops of hills so that runners could not be easily seen by enemy tribes. Occasionally an Indian path opened out on a meadow or forest clearing, or crossed another path. In these places native Americans sometimes met to trade with one another. Later, when European traders came to the Indian lands, they traded with the natives at the same spots.

There were several important Indian trails. To the north was the **Iroquois Trail.** This route ran from the Hudson River west along the Mohawk River to Lake Erie. This area would become part of the state of New York. South of the Iroquois Trail was the **Kittanning Path.** This trail ran from eastern Pennsylvania over the Appalachian Mountains through Kittanning Gorge. From there, the road continued to the Allegheny River, which flows into the great Ohio River. A later road built by the English followed this old Indian trail. **Forbes's Road** was constructed for travel to Fort Duquesne (later called Fort Pitt and, today, Pittsburgh) during the time of the French and Indian War.

The **Warriors' Path** was another important Indian road. This route had several different branches. It ran, basically, from North Carolina to Ohio. But its branches stretched into Virginia and Kentucky. Daniel Boone, the great American **trailblazer,** used the Warriors' Path to create a road in the 1750s. The Warriors' Path also included a branch which followed the course of the Ohio River, running westward from Kentucky and making its way to St. Louis, Missouri. It did not, however, run consistently parallel with the Ohio all the way to St. Louis.

Some tribes used the trail system to travel great distances. Some raiding parties of Plains Indians traveled as far as 2,000 miles from their homes. Back east, Iroquois braves, ranging out from their villages in New

★

York, brought back Sioux captives from as far away as what is now South Dakota. The Iroquois also fought nations as far south as Florida.

Without a doubt, the vast Indian path system allowed tribes to stay in contact with one another. The trails allowed Indians to trade and wage war. In fact, native Americans from the Atlantic to the Pacific oceans probably communicated through the trail system. This contact brought about the use of sign language. Signs could be understood by tribes of many nations, even though they spoke hundreds of different languages and dialects. But the native American trails and paths, as well as the buffalo highways, also brought European settlers into contact with the Indians. Unfortunately, this contact often led to fighting between the two groups.

Colonial Roads

When the first European colonists came to America, they found their new lives difficult. They faced problems with the native Americans, with the weather and with finding enough food to eat. These early colonials fought disease and starvation. But among all these difficulties was another one: the problem of getting around without good roads.

Because the colonists huddled along the Atlantic coast, they did not use the great Indian trail system that crisscrossed the interior of the continent. They settled along the many rivers from Maine to Georgia. For the first 150 years of colonizing, nearly every settlement was built along a river. Colonists could travel along these water routes easily. These river systems connected the colonists with sailing ships from England, France and other European countries. They also provided rich soil for farming. For many decades, few colonials had any reason to build long road systems. Most colonists became interested in roads that could connect one town to another. The colonials did use the local American Indian trails when they could. But these trails did not always connect the new settlements to one another. Thus, roads needed to be built.

As early as 1639, leaders in Massachusetts decided that a road should be built between the village of Plymouth (where the Pilgrims had landed in 1620) and the town of Boston. But even that road was no more than a mere path. There were very few wheeled vehicles in America at that early date. Almost all road or trail traffic was on foot or on horseback.

Down south in colonial Virginia, travel on paths and roads was also developing. By 1689, Virginia had nearly 60,000 people. Most of them stayed in contact along the rivers. But land routes were being made, too. Indian paths were widened by greater use. Still, the early Virginia roads were poor and narrow. Travel by vehicle over long distances was nearly impossible. In fact, not until around 1750 did actual road building begin seriously in America. By that time, the first wheeled vehicles and **sedan chairs** were in use in the colonies.

The Army Builds Two Roads

In the 1750s, two important roads were built by British soldiers. During that decade, England and France were at war in Europe. They were also fighting in America. The French had built forts in Canada. They claimed the great **Ohio Valley,** the land west of the Appalachians and north of the Ohio River, as French. The British said that area was English property. To help claim the Ohio Valley, the French built a fort in western Pennsylvania at

★

The roads developed by the British army were eventually
used by American pioneers searching for western settlements.

★

the headwaters of the Ohio River. They called it Fort Duquesne.

In 1755 a large British army marched into the western wilderness toward Fort Duquesne. This army was led by General Edward Braddock. The army followed a narrow road which had been built by a trading company just three years earlier. But Braddock's troops and some Virginia militia made the road longer and better. They extended it all the way to Fort Duquesne. This road was important to later colonists because it allowed them to travel from the Virginia coast to the Ohio River. A half-century later, a section of this route became part of the **National Road,** which you will read about later.

After Braddock cut his road through the wilderness in 1755, he was defeated by the French in battle. Three years later, a second British army marched on the fort from eastern Pennsylvania. Led by General John Forbes, this force of 6,500 troops moved along a road built from Lancaster, Pennsylvania, to Fort Duquesne. Fourteen hundred soldiers were used to carve the road out of the wilderness. For the next 30 years, Forbes's Road was the most important highway from the East to the Ohio Valley. It was used in the 1790s as a freight route for **Conestoga wagons,** large covered wagons that carried several tons of goods.

Both Braddock's Road and Forbes's Road helped to establish routes for people wanting to go west. Once these early highways were built, thousands of people poured into the Ohio Valley. These roads continued to be improved and widened as the decades passed and traffic grew.

★

Daniel Boone
and the
Wilderness Road

S ome colonists began to consider exploring the lands west of the Appalachian Mountains. Many land-hungry colonists, fed up with strict control from the English government, were set to move west. Stories were already being told about the great open meadows of Kentucky, ready to be broken by the plow. But a road was needed if entire families were going to pack up and move to the rich farmlands of Kentucky and Tennessee.

The man who helped open up these western lands was the famous trailblazer Daniel Boone. Born in 1734 in Pennsylvania, he grew up in the wilderness. As a boy, he made friends and hunted with members of the nearby Indian tribe. From them he learned the ways of the woods and frontier. In 1750 the Boone family moved to North Carolina. Daniel shot game for the family table.

Daniel Boone became a famous American trailblazer who inspired the nation's early settlers to explore western lands.

At age 20, Boone worked as a wagon driver during Braddock's march toward Fort Duquesne. While on that march, he heard stories about the rich land of Kentucky. He listened to people who claimed that so many turkeys lived in "Kaintuck," they could not all fly at the same time. Boone heard the stories and longed to go and see this great natural paradise.

More than ten years were to pass before Daniel Boone had his chance to visit Kentucky. By then he was married and had a growing family. He and his wife had to farm to feed their children. But when a peddler passed by his farm in 1768, Boone's dream of Kentucky began to take shape. The peddler was an old friend of his from the Braddock campaign. The man, named John Finley, had learned of an Indian trail, called the Warriors' Path, that led to Kentucky. He talked Boone into following him to the western territory. Boone was ready to go.

In May of 1769, Boone and a party of five men set out along the Warriors' Path, headed for Kentucky. They pushed through the wilderness for a month until they passed through the mountains. Then, on June 7, the six woodsmen reached the great hunting valley of "Kentucke." Boone and the others saw a rich country, filled with buffalo and deer. They saw a land watered by a winding river. They knew they had discovered the path to something special.

For nearly two years, Boone and his friends stayed in Kentucky. They shot wild game and explored the region. Some of the men were killed by Indians, and Boone himself was captured. He managed to escape, however, and finally returned to his family and friends in North Carolina in March 1771. Now it was Daniel Boone who told the stories about the richness of Kentucky. His tales spread from North Carolina into Virginia. Soon peo-

★

ple were preparing to pack up their belongings and head west. In 1773, Boone, his family and several others started for the western lands. But Indians attacked and killed several men, including Boone's oldest son, James. After this attack, the pioneer group turned back.

Blazing the Wilderness Road

In 1775, a North Carolina judge named Richard Henderson wanted to build a colony in Kentucky. He formed a company, called the **Transylvania Company** ("transylvania" is a word meaning "through the woods"), to buy land for the colony from the Cherokee Indians. He hired the well-known Daniel Boone to go into the area and build a better road for pioneer families to travel on into Kentucky. If Boone were successful, he would be making the first road through the wilderness.

Boone the Trailblazer

Boone headed west with about 30 explorers. He and his party started out from Fort Wautaga as soon as the Cherokee Indians had agreed to sell a part of their land. Pack horses carried the equipment. The group, however, carried axes. Boone led the way into the wilderness. As he walked along, he cut deep notches into large trees with his tomahawk. These marks were called blazes. Since Boone and his party were creating a line or trail behind them as they went, what they were doing was called "blazing the way" or "trailblazing."

The road Boone made was not entirely original. He followed the old Indian route called the Warriors' Path. At some points he left the ancient trail and followed a wide "buffalo street." In other places he carved his own trail entirely. By April 15, 1775, Boone and his

★

party had completed their tasks. The Wilderness Road was finished. Along the south bank of the Kentucky River, they built a fort, which they called Boonesborough. The fort measured about 250 feet by 150 feet. At each corner, a blockhouse was built. Rows of sharpened logs stood upright, forming the fort's walls. Inside, rows of log cabins were constructed. The fort was completed on June 14.

Boonesborough was the fort that Daniel Boone and his party built in Kentucky.

★

By the end of the year 1775, several hundred pioneers had moved into Kentucky along Boone's Wilderness Road. He had succeeded in creating the first primitive road into the Kentucky region. But what kind of road was it? It was nothing like a modern road. It was difficult to travel and was not wide enough for wagons. It was the route Boone had followed that was important. He had used existing Indian and buffalo trails, as well as some trails of his own making. The result was a new path, used by people new to the Kentucky region.

For the first time, pioneers were ready to settle permanently in the wide-open region they called "Kentucke." While some colonists were busy fighting the British during the American Revolution, thousands of pioneers headed for Kentucky. By 1784, 30,000 people had arrived in the western territory. That summer alone, 12,000 Americans migrated to Kentucky, ready to begin new lives in a new country.

As more and more people used Boone's Wilderness Road, other routes and branches were traced. An early road called the **Tennessee Path** soon ran into northern Tennessee. Other Kentucky branches spread across the territory. These branches connected with and crisscrossed each other. One ran to the new settlement of Louisville, Kentucky, on the Ohio River. This road later extended to Vincennes, Indiana, and then on west to St. Louis. In 1795, the Kentucky lawmakers passed a bill called "An act opening a Wagon Road to Cumberland Gap." This law hoped to create a route, following Boone's Wilderness Road, that wagons could use. In just a few years, work on the road was complete. A wagon could pass through the Cumberland Gap and follow Boone's road all the way to Crab Orchard, Kentucky, in the center of the state. (Kentucky had become a state in 1792.)

★

Other Trails
Develop

Other trails leading into the western territories developed at the same time. A trail connecting Baltimore, Maryland, with Redstone, Pennsylvania (today called Brownsville), began to take shape and became an important wagon road. From Richmond, Virginia, a path led northwest through the upper Shenandoah Valley until it connected with the Baltimore-Redstone trail. Each of these paths led into the Ohio country, which was opening up to pioneers just as Kentucky and Tennessee were.

In 1796 the U.S. Congress gave President Washington the power to contract Ebenezer Zane to carve a trail or trace through Ohio. Zane, who lived on the Maryland side of the Potomac River, began to cut his trail from Wheeling, Virginia (today, West Virginia), across southeast Ohio. His trail crossed the **Seven Ranges,** the part of Ohio which was first surveyed. On the banks of the Muskingum River in Ohio, a settlement called Zanesville would eventually be built. Zane himself later established a ferry there, which crossed the

★

Muskingum. From there, Zane progressed southwest. He finally finished his trail after reaching the Ohio River and the Kentucky River settlement of Limestone. Zane's Trace gave Ohio pioneers a trail to follow into the western territory. Later, a part of Zane's Trace was used in building the National Road.

Roads Back East

While different western roads were being blazed in territories from Ohio to Tennessee, colonists along the Atlantic coast were building new roads of their own. As the colonies grew, many wheeled vehicles were being used. These carts, wagons and carriages required better roads. More and more people were traveling from one colony to another. Cities such as Philadelphia, Boston, New York and Baltimore were trying to stay in touch with each other. The people in the colonies worked to see that roads were improved and extended.

Earlier in the 18th century, private individuals or companies built roads. They also built bridges across rivers and streams. Some of the early road construction began with bridge building. These privately built bridges were **toll bridges,** meaning anyone using them was charged a few cents for the privilege. As early as 1730, the first toll bridges were built. In the beginning, such bridges were built on only a few important roads. But they were profitable, and more were built.

By the 1790s more roads and bridges were being built by hundreds of private companies. Most states were not very involved in such construction. The new roads were called turnpikes or **toll roads.** Since they were built by private citizens, the builders wanted to make a profit. So, just like toll bridges, anyone using a toll road had to pay.

★

Although they may have looked different, colonial toll roads and bridges worked very much like the present-day versions.

★

These private companies completed most of their road building between 1795 and 1810. Over 170 turnpike companies were in business in New England alone during those years. They spent over $5 million building or improving nearly 3,000 miles of road.

Construction of roads in New England was expensive. Building costs went up according to how difficult the road was to build. A New England road might cost anywhere from $200 to $13,000 per mile in the 18th and 19th centuries! New roads might be priced higher because the company often had to buy more land. The number of bridges a company had to build on a road increased the cost dramatically. Most New England roads did not have an even surface because the soil was so sandy.

Other regions joined the trend. New York, for example, had 88 companies building another 3,000 miles of road by 1807. Pennsylvania, by 1821, had just as many companies as New York, working on over 1,800 miles of road. In those states such privately built roads were often made using gravel beds.

Because of the development of toll roads and turnpikes in the years following the American Revolu-

Conestogas were strong wagons that were able to carry heavy loads.

tion, life changed for the average American. Such roads allowed for the development of the stagecoach system. Between 1800 and 1830 both stagecoaches and privately owned carriages and wagons were using the turnpikes in greater numbers. Cities and towns, as well as small, remote villages, were brought closer together.

By 1850 most roads in America were free for the public to use. Toll-road companies were going out of business. Other forms of transportation, such as canals, early railroads and steamboats, were giving the private roads too much competition. Even as early as 1825, turnpike stocks were becoming worthless. These private roads had proven too costly, in the long run, to make an annual profit.

Lancaster Pike

During this period of private turnpikes, one of the most important was the **Lancaster Pike.** In fact, it was the first turnpike in America. Construction began in 1791, and the road was opened to travel in 1797. This turnpike connected Philadelphia with the trading center of Lancaster, Pennsylvania. The idea for a turnpike had been discussed as early as 1770, before the Revolutionary War. But with the coming of the war, the plan was put on the shelf. When the idea was revived in the 1780s, a company was formed. The Philadelphia and Lancaster Turnpike Road Company offered stock to the public to help pay for the new road.

What made the Lancaster Pike different from other American roads of its day was the way it was built. Most roads built in the United States were simply made of dirt. When the rains came, these primitive roads became muddy and difficult to use. However, cities had been using a "hard road" process for years. Early city streets used **cobblestones,** which were large, smooth pebbles. Later streets were paved with **road metal,** a combination of gravel or crushed stone and sand and clay. The Lancaster Pike's engineers used a method similar to the road-metal approach.

The Lancaster Pike roadbed used crushed rock of less than 1 inch in diameter. This was spread on a stone foundation at least 10 inches deep. The pike was built wide enough to allow two lanes of wagon traffic. For 60 miles, it stretched west to Philadelphia, a masterpiece of American road construction. The company spent $465,000 building the pike, but the changes it brought to western trade and travel made it worth all the money invested.

Great numbers of stagecoaches, carriages and special freight wagons—the Conestogas—traveled the new road, and a 12-hour night stage service began in the spring of 1798 between Lancaster and Philadelphia. The federal government saw the need for other such roads. More and more people were going west to the **Northwest Territory**

★

The Need for a New Road

Since the carving of Zane's Trace, western travelers could jump off from Wheeling, West Virginia, to the Ohio country. But to get to Zane's Trace, travelers first had to reach Wheeling, a difficult trip by way of Cumberland, Maryland. A road was necessary. After much debate in the U.S. Congress, an act was passed in 1802 which gave Ohio its statehood. Part of this act allowed for the building of an east-west road. This road was to become the National or Cumberland Road. In 1806 the federal government decided to run the road from the Atlantic Ocean to the Mississippi River.

True construction of the road did not begin until 1808. The route started in Maryland and did not reach the Ohio border, at Wheeling, until 1818. The first leg of the road was built between Baltimore and Cumberland and was finished in 1814.

The road did not move very far west for several years after that. Survey work did not begin in Ohio, Indiana and Illinois until 1820. Construction did not start

★

Many trees were cut down during the construction of the National Road.

★

in these states until 1825. The road reached Columbus, Ohio, in 1833. It ran into Indiana by 1837 and hit the Illinois border in 1850. From there, paved road construction ended and the road continued across the Illinois prairie on to St. Louis, unpaved.

Building the National Road

Construction of this important road required a great amount of planning and work. The driving surface of the road was 30 feet wide, very broad for a road of that day. This width was to allow for two-way wagon and stagecoach traffic. The road was paved with an inch of crushed stone and a layer of gravel laid on top of it. As often as possible the builders followed a level route. Little road grading was done, as it took much time and money. Trees that measured 18 inches or less around were cut down, leaving 9-inch-high stumps. Larger trees, measuring greater than 18 inches, were cut at 15 inches high. Many of these stumps were left right in the middle of the road! To make them less hazardous to wagon and carriage traffic, the stumps were rounded and trimmed. Pull-offs were built along both sides of the highway. Measuring 25 feet wide each, these side strips allowed wagons to park alongside the road for repairs, rest or overnight camping.

Traffic on the National Road

From 1827 until about 1850, the National Road (also called the Cumberland Road or the United States Road) was the most popular road in America. Traffic flowed both east and west on the road. Pioneers traveled west in large numbers. Farmers and traders hauled their goods to markets in the East.

In time, there were many different ways to travel on the National Road. But three types were most often found on the route. These were Conestoga freight-wagon trains, stagecoaches and mule or horse pack trains.

Conestogas Carry Goods

When Conestoga wagons rolled along the National Road, they were hard to miss; there were so many of them on the road. These wagons were very large. The wagons' beds measured about 10 feet long and nearly 4 feet wide. The beds curved up on both ends to keep goods from spilling out. The Conestogas were topped by great white canvas covers held up by curved wooden bows. These heavy wagons had wheels 5 feet high, banded with iron. They were painted bright red and blue. Six massive German-bred horses, called Conestogas (although there was no such breed), pulled the large wagons. The horses often had bells attached to their harnesses. As the wagons rolled along, the bells rang, telling people a Conestoga caravan was headed their way. These wagons were used to carry 6 tons of freight to neighboring towns. Because the wagons were so heavy, they traveled only about 2 miles an hour.

★

Riding in a stagecoach was the quickest and most comfortable way to travel along the National Road.

The Speedy Stagecoach

The first four-horse stagecoach to travel the National Road from Baltimore arrived in Pittsburgh on August 1, 1817. Stagecoaches were the fastest way of traveling on the National Road. The coaches followed day and night schedules. They changed horses every 12 miles or so to keep the teams from wearing out. Changing horses at a stage house was done quickly; in fact, the new team was often hitched up in about a minute. Coach travel was more expensive than other means of getting around on the National Road. It usually cost $17.25 to ride the stage from Baltimore to Wheeling, unless the traveler was an important person, such as a senator or judge. Then the stage-line owner marked the person's hat with a piece of chalk. Drivers understood that such a mark meant that the person rode the line for free.

American stagecoaches had been redesigned from older models just about the time the National Road was open for business. Older stages had been built on S-springs, giving passengers and drivers alike a very bumpy ride. Later coaches rested the coach body on

★

leather straps. This allowed the coach to "float" rather than jolt. But while the straps gave the passengers a less shocking ride, the swaying motion made some people sick.

Stagecoaches on the National Road could carry nine passengers in three rows of three. Luggage was tied to the rear of the coach, and sometimes extra baggage was lashed to the roof. The driver did not sit on the coach roof but on a seat attached to the front of the coach body. A team of four horses pulled the coach along the road at an average speed of 5 to 6 miles an hour. When a stage had a special message to deliver (such as the election of a new president), the driver drove an often empty stage at high speed, flying along at rates of 10 to 12 miles an hour!

Pack Trains Encourage Trade

When thousands of Americans moved into the frontier, they took with them most of what they needed to live. But these early farmers, herders and trappers could not supply themselves with everything necessary for living in the wilderness. People needed lead and gunpowder for their rifles and muskets. They needed salt to season their food and to preserve meats. On occasion, they needed store-bought goods, such as sugar, tobacco and cloth.

Since most people in America at that time did not have much actual money, they needed to get things by trading. Settlers on the frontier could go to a town or city and exchange western goods, such as furs, deer hides, bear grease, cord wood, crops and even ashes from burned wood (which were used by soap makers, papermakers, dyers and tanners), for the things they needed.

★

Early Americans relied upon the work provided by pack train service.

Pack trains often carried wilderness produce to market. In the fall, pioneer settlements provided horses or mules for a community pack train. They loaded the animals with the goods and sent them back east, where the goods were to be sold or traded. Often such a pack train consisted of 12 to 15 horses, tethered together in single file. Only two people were needed to lead the horse train to market. Pack trains were a common sight along the National Road and other routes.

Each pack train was slightly different, but most followed the same pattern. Small, sure-footed horses were used. Every horse had a bell hung around its neck. While on the road, the bells were tied down, making them silent. Only when a pack train was coming into a town or settlement, ready to trade, were the bell clappers let loose. Then a pack train entered a village "with bells on," announcing to the local people that the train

★

was in town. The bell clappers were also loosened at night while the horses grazed. This made it easier to find the horses the next morning.

The pack trains carried more than just produce and goods to sell and trade. The leaders of the pack train had to carry food for the horses and for themselves. Foods that could keep without refrigeration were taken for the packers to eat: beef jerky, smoked bacon, cheese and johnnycakes or hoecakes, which were thin cakes made of cornmeal. Pack trains also carried the mail from back home. Many pioneer families had relatives back east and used such trains to send letters to them.

Along the National Road, packers might stay overnight in an ordinary (a wayside inn and tavern). Here they could get a place to sleep and a hot meal. The packers slept on the floor of such places, with many snoring bodies crowded all over a fire-lit room. With such sleeping arrangements, the safest place was under a table, where a traveler was less likely to get stepped on.

On return trips west, pack trains brought back a different cargo. There were answered letters from relatives. Sometimes new settlers joined the returning train. Salt was stored and carried in bags. Iron or lead bars for bullets and gun making were bent into U-shapes and fitted over the backs of horses. Cooking pots, skillets, knives, tools, pewter dishes, loaves of sugar and dress material, called calico, often rounded out the returning cargo.

As more and more pioneers ventured west, the amount of produce for market grew. Eventually, professional packers or **drovers** contracted with wilderness settlements to haul their goods for a fee.

★

Far Western Trails and Routes

During the years 1820-1860 Americans east of the Mississippi River were busy building new roads. These roads, such as the National Road, opened up the eastern states to settlement and trade. But at the same time, trails were opening up the territories west of the Mississippi. These trails and roads could be found from Oregon in the Pacific Northwest to the southwestern settlement of Santa Fe. Some of the routes were discovered by mountaineers and fur trappers. Others were expanded and improved from ancient American Indian paths and Spanish trails. Among the most important western trails were the Santa Fe Trail, the Oregon and California trails, and various western stagecoach roads.

The Santa Fe Trail

The Santa Fe trail connected settlers in Missouri with Mexican traders in the town of Santa Fe, in what is today the state of New Mexico. The most important trade

American pioneers loaded goods on pack trains for trading along the Santa Fe Trail.

period for Americans using the Santa Fe Trail was from 1821 to 1880. Most Anglo-Americans who used the trail before 1821 were not well received. The colonial Spanish government frowned on Americans moving into their northern outpost of Santa Fe. Spanish officials arrested the great American military explorer Zebulon Pike near Santa Fe in 1807, while he was on a mapping expedition in the Southwest. Trade with Santa Fe was not possible at that time for traders from America.

The Mexican people overthrew their Spanish leaders in 1821. Only then did Santa Fe open its doors to Americans. One of the first to travel there was a Missourian named William Becknell. He arrived in Santa Fe on November 16. He traded with the Santa Fe natives and made a great profit from his goods.

Before Becknell's trip to Santa Fe from Missouri, the route of the Santa Fe Trail was not well defined. Becknell started out from Franklin, Missouri, and crossed the prairie between the Kansas and Arkansas rivers. About 200 miles out, Becknell began following the Arkansas River. Once he arrived at the foothills of the southern Rocky Mountains, he turned southwest, cutting across the southeast corner of what is today Colorado. Bent's Fort was later built at that turning point. From there Becknell continued southwest until he arrived in the frontier settlement of Santa Fe. Becknell's route was to become the Santa Fe Trail of history.

Over the years, U.S. traders followed the trail in caravans or wagon trains. They used large Conestoga wagons. These wagons were rarely used west of the Mississippi River. But the flat desert land was suitable for the heavy freight wagons. They moved in long parallel columns, which were formed into circles at night. Indian attack was always a possibility along the trail, but few traders ever faced hostile natives.

★

The peak year for American trade along the trail was 1843. At that time, nearly $500,000 worth of goods were carried in wagons on the trail. The year which saw the largest number of people and wagons on the trail was 1848-1849. That year, 3,000 wagons, 12,000 people and 50,000 animals used the trail. Most of the people, however, did not follow the trail all the way to Santa Fe. They were on their way to California to look for gold. Stagecoach service was established along the trail in 1849, as well. When the Atchison, Topeka and Santa Fe railroad was opened in 1880, the old wagon road became less and less important as a trade route.

The Oregon and California Trails

During the late 1830s and 1840s, many Americans were eager to move into the vast Oregon country and to the gold camps of California. For travel there by wagon, the Oregon Trail became the most popular emigrant road west of the Mississippi. The road began as a trail first used by Indians, then by fur trappers and traders. As early as 1805, the Lewis and Clark expedition had covered part of what was to later become the famous pioneer highway. In 1812, fur trappers led by Robert Stuart covered much of the trail. But these trappers followed the trail from Oregon back east to Missouri, the jumping-off place for western pioneers.

Once missionaries had taken the trail to Oregon, alongside fur-trapping mountain people, whole families of easterners began packing up and taking wagons on the Oregon Trail. The trail began at Independence, Missouri, and coursed west near the Kansas River. The route turned northwest until pioneers found themselves traveling across Nebraska along the Platte and North

★

Platte rivers. Wagon trains then crossed the Rocky Mountains at the South Pass.

Soon the trail split into two roads. At Soda Springs, in today's Idaho, settlers bound for Oregon went on to the northwest. California-seekers splintered off and went to the southwest, north of the Great Salt Lake, in Utah. Oregon people passed through more mountains, followed the Snake River, and finally found themselves along the banks of the Columbia River. From there they followed the river until they arrived in the Willamette Valley. Here they could find rich farmland and start their new lives out west.

Those travelers who chose the California Trail cut across open country to the Humboldt River in the eastern part of modern-day Nevada. This difficult passage took pioneers through the desert and into the Sierra Nevada. Once the California-seekers had crossed the mountains, the gold camps lay ahead.

These pioneer trails brought hundreds of thousands of Americans to the Pacific territories of California and Oregon. The settlers were very important to the growth and building of western towns and cities.

Western Stagecoach Lines

When gold was discovered in 1848, many people back east were in a hurry to get to California. By the summer of 1849, a stagecoach line was in operation between Independence, Missouri, and Santa Fe. In 1850 another line, between Independence and Salt Lake City, Utah, was opened. Coaches on this line made monthly trips. A later stage road was opened in 1857 between San Antonio, Texas, and San Diego, California. These coaches were required to complete each one-way trip within a time limit of 30 days. In just a few years, stagecoach lines were busy across thousands of miles of the West.

In 1858, one of the most famous lines was in operation. It was called the Southern Overland Mail line. Its owner was a man named John Butterfield. The line opened in September 1857, and it followed a long oxbow-shaped route from Tipton, Missouri, all the way to San Francisco. (Most of the great gold camps were near San Francisco.) This route ran southwest through Fort Smith, Arkansas, across Indian territory and Texas. From there the stages went through El Paso, Texas, Tucson, Arizona, and San Diego. A later branch of this line ran from Fort Smith back east to Memphis, Tennessee.

Western travel on a stagecoach was generally the same everywhere. Stages rattled along at an average speed of 120 miles in 24 hours of travel. This meant a speed of about 5 miles an hour. When the coaches ran through sandy or muddy roads or went uphill, the speed was cut to 3 miles an hour or less. If a stage on the Southern Overland stayed on schedule, the trip from St. Louis to San Francisco took about 24 days. And for the privilege of being bounced halfway across the country, passengers paid $150-$200 one way.

Stage crews on the Butterfield route usually consisted of a driver and a conductor. Drivers rode the stagecoach over a 65-mile route. At the end of that distance, the driver changed coaches and rode back over the same route. By doing this, drivers came to know their routes very well. In fact, this is what allowed them to drive the routes at night. The conductor was in charge of the coach, as well as the passengers, mail and anything else the stage might be carrying. Conductors were not limited to the same short routes as the drivers. Most conductors stayed on the stagecoaches

★

for several hundred miles. Both drivers and conductors carried guns. Much of the Butterfield route ran through Indian lands. And there was always the possibility of stagecoach robbers.

Such stagecoach routes helped to link the West Coast with the eastern part of the country. They cut the travel time between these areas to just a few weeks. (Most pioneer wagon trains took six months to cover the western lands.) They helped to establish later routes for railroads and western automobile highways.

A trip in a stagecoach across the Southern Overland Mail route was usually a long and unpleasant experience for the passengers.

★

Modern roadways and vehicles make it easy to travel across the country today.

★

American Roads
Today

L ook at any road map of the United States today and you will realize just how important the early roads in the young United States were. Many of those routes are still used today. Some superhighways today follow the same courses that buffalo took hundreds of years ago. Rail lines, automobile roads, even airline routes still use the paths first taken by native Americans, from the Atlantic to the Pacific.

Travel by wagon, stagecoach, pack train or carriage was very slow. It took an immigrant family months to reach their new home. Today, people get into their cars and travel to places hundreds of miles away in just one day. But the early roads and trails did help the United States to grow and reach out across the continent. The roads forged by early pioneers, traders and travelers caused the United States to become a great nation stretching across mountains, prairies and deserts, from ocean to ocean.

★

For Further Reading

Davies, Eryl. *Transport on Land, Road & Rail.* New York: Franklin Watts, 1992.

Greene, Carol. *Daniel Boone: Man of the Forests.* Chicago: Childrens Press, 1990.

Tunis, Edwin. *Colonial Living.* New York: HarperCollins Children's Books, 1976.

Tunis, Edwin. *Frontier Living.* New York: HarperCollins Children's Books, 1976.

Tunis, Edwin. *Wheels: A Pictorial History.* New York: HarperCollins Children's Books, 1977.

The roads and transportation systems developed by colonists and pioneers helped to build the nation as we know it today.

Glossary

cobblestone—A naturally rounded stone used to pave streets.

Conestoga wagon—A covered wagon with a large sloping bed, used by American pioneers to haul freight.

drover—Pack-mule driver; a person who led pack mules.

Forbes's Road—A road built by British soldiers under the command of General John Forbes. The road ran from Lancaster, Pennsylvania, to Fort Duquesne (later called Pittsburgh).

Iroquois Trail—Lengthy Indian trail, or path, which ran along the Mohawk River in upstate New York from Albany to Lake Erie.

Kittanning Path—Indian trail running from eastern Pennsylvania over the Appalachian Mountains, through Kittanning Gorge to the Allegheny River.

Lancaster Pike—The first important turnpike road in America. People using the road had to pay for the privilege. The road ran from Philadelphia to Lancaster, Pennsylvania, about 60 miles west. It was built in the 1790s.

National Road—The government-financed road running from Maryland to Wheeling, West Virginia, built beginning in 1808. In later years the road was extended to Ohio, then Indiana, and finally to Illinois.

Northwest Territory—The area between the Ohio and Mississippi rivers. The states of Ohio, Indiana, Illinois, Michigan and Wisconsin were carved out of the territory.

Ohio Valley—The western land bordered by the Great Lakes to the north, the Appalachian Mountains to the east, the Mississippi River to the west and the Gulf Coast to the south.

road metal—A combination of gravel or crushed stones and sand or clay.

salt lick—A natural place where salt is found on the surface of the ground; animals go there to lick the salt.

sedan chair—A covered chair made to carry one person. Two people used poles to lift the chair.

Seven Ranges—The first part of the Northwest Territory to be surveyed under the Ordinance of 1785. The Seven Ranges formed a triangle with a western boundary 91 miles in length, a northern one of 42 miles and the Ohio River as the third side.

Tennessee Path—An early pioneer road running from Kentucky into northern Tennessee.

toll bridge—A bridge built by a private citizen or company, which people could use only after they paid a fee, or toll.

toll road—A road which could be used only after a person paid a fee, or toll.

trailblazer—A pioneer, such as Daniel Boone, who made a new trail into the wilderness. (The word "blaze" referred to the notches carved into trees to mark the route for those who might follow.)

Transylvania Company—A land-speculation company that hired Daniel Boone to explore and build a road into the wilderness of Kentucky.

Warriors' Path—An American Indian war road, used by both northern and southern Indian nations, which ran through Kentucky and the Cumberland Gap.

Index

★